STREETS OF STRUGGLE

Terry Hords

Table of Contents

CHAPTER 1:
SEEDS OF STRUGGLE

In the depths of my memory lies a story that began when I was just a child—a story of struggles, triumphs, and the resilience of the human spirit. From my earliest days, I was plagued by seizures, a challenge that many people face even today.

I have experienced firsthand what it's like to have seizures - all types. Growing up, I would be playing one moment, and then suddenly, without warning, I'd feel this peculiar sensation in my body, dizziness creeping in, and everything around me appearing strange. Before I knew it, I'd collapse and have a seizure. It was a challenging experience for me and my mother, who always worried about my well-being.

Back then, I struggled to remember to take my pills, and as a kid, I would sometimes even hide them in my room. But hiding the pills didn't help. Seizures could still strike unexpectedly. Sometimes, I would feel a strange aura before a seizure hit - like a funny feeling crawling on my skin. It was unsettling. I'd lose control during these episodes, like the world was slipping away.

I remember one incident when I had a seizure; it was like the walls were closing in on me. It was terrifying, but somehow, they stopped before they crushed me, freezing in place like a surreal tableau. I felt stuck in the middle of it all, with no escape. Fortunately, there were people around who knew how to handle these situations. They'd hold my tongue with a spoon or something similar to prevent me from accidentally biting it during the seizure.

Once the paramedics arrived, they'd provide the necessary medical attention. But recovering from a seizure wasn't a quick process. It left a profound impact on my memory. After such episodes, my memory would be hazy for months, and it would take a while to regain my cognitive abilities fully.

The struggle with seizures took a toll on me emotionally and mentally. I'd find it hard to remember things I had learned at school, making academic life quite challenging. But with the support of my loved ones and medical professionals, I gradually found ways to cope and adapt to this condition.

Living with seizures has been a journey filled with ups and downs, but I've learned to cherish the good times and persevere through the difficult ones. It's been a journey of understanding myself, accepting my condition, and finding the strength to carry on despite the obstacles it brings. And with each passing day, I continue to grow and be responsible, learning to appreciate the beauty of life, even with its challenges.

As a child of seven or eight, my mother imparted vital lessons about responsibility. She knew she couldn't be by my side forever, so she taught me to take my medications diligently. I remember experiencing seizures that seemed like a raging fire closing in on me while others left me helpless, struggling to swallow.

Throughout my youth, my mother became my constant companion on trips to various doctors, hospitals, and emergency rooms. The journey was challenging, but her unwavering support carried me through.

An event that changed my life forever marked the first time I ever witnessed a tragedy unfold before my eyes. The incident involved a boy getting killed right before me, a chilling experience for a young soul like mine, merely 14 years old at the time.

You see, there was this guy named John, a childhood friend of mine, and we grew up together, and he always carried around a gun, flashing it often to remind me that he could protect me if needed. But deep down, I knew this wasn't right, and I constantly urged him to keep the gun away, particularly when we were out and about in our neighborhood.

One day, things took a tragic turn. A 13-year-old boy had just moved into our neighborhood. He attempted to take apart John's bike, and when John found out about it, he got furious. My instincts kicked in, and I tried to reason with him, telling him that violence wasn't the answer. But John seemed possessed by anger and wouldn't listen to anyone except me, his friend.

As the situation escalated, John grabbed his gun, but initially, he didn't have any bullets loaded. I pleaded with him again to put the gun away and not resort to violence. He seemed to heed my advice and returned inside, seemingly putting the gun away. But when he returned, he had loaded the gun with bullets. It was as if the world slowed as I witnessed the sequence of events.

Tragically, John shot the boy, and panic erupted. People started running, and I couldn't fully grasp what happened. The little boy tried to get back up on his bike, but his strength failed him, and he fell to the ground, dying before our eyes. It was a devastating sight, etched into my memory forever.

During those dark times, I found support from my family, especially my mother, who was there for me despite dealing with her grief. Their love and care helped me cope as I grew older, but the scars from those incidents continue to linger, shaping the person I am today.

Looking back, it's hard to believe that all of this happened during a school break when I was about to enter high school. The neighborhood I grew up in was tough, and such tragedies were unfortunately not uncommon. It's a story that shaped my life, leaving an indelible mark on my soul, and one that I believe carries vital lessons for others to understand and empathize with the struggles that many of us face in our journey through life.

My family had its ups and downs during my younger years, but overall, it felt like a relationship - not a bad one, but one with moments of tension. For instance, things changed when my oldest brother and my mother passed away. I found myself seeking comfort and support from my sister Babe, spending nights at her house before returning to my oldest brother's place, where I was staying at the time. The relationship with my family, including my sisters and brothers, was okay, but the absence of our mother left a void, and sometimes, loneliness crept in.

However, fate dealt me a devastating blow when I turned 16. First, my beloved brother lost his life tragically, leaving a void that could never be filled. Then, only three months later, my world crumbled once again as my mother succumbed to breast cancer. Their passing left me empty, but I found solace in the memories of how my brother had been my guardian angel during my seizures. His swift and calming actions saved me from the brink of danger, holding my tongue to prevent injury until help arrived. But now, with both my brother and mother gone, I was left to face my challenges alone.

Yet, the heartache from losing my support system weighed heavily on me. My brother and mother, my angels on earth, had been my saviors, guiding me through life's most trying moments. With their absence, I knew I had to take charge of my destiny and be more self-reliant, despite having siblings who cared deeply for me.

Despite the challenges, I still had a pretty good relationship with my family. My siblings were there for me, and we had no major issues. Even after my mother's passing, the bond remained strong. The support and connection with my sisters and brothers helped me navigate difficult times.

Reflecting on my relationship with my siblings, I recall various experiences. For instance, my sister Babe and I had a decent relationship; I would visit her house and spend time together.

Similarily, my relationship with my sister Cookie was also okay, despite its ups and downs.

Sometimes, I'd visit my older brother's house and return to my sister's place. It felt like a constant back-and-forth, but it was part of the routine.

During my teenage years, around 1987, there were times when I felt unwanted by my oldest brother and his wife. They didn't seem eager to have me around, but my mother insisted I stay with them. This situation caused some discomfort and tension. I could sense that his wife didn't fully embrace my presence, which made me feel a bit out of place.

Despite these occasional challenges, I forged my path and became more independent. As time went on, I learned to navigate my family dynamics, and I cherished the positive relationships that formed with my siblings. While there were moments of difficulty, I believe those experiences shaped me into the person I am today, and I hold no grudges or ill feelings toward anyone. My family, in its unique way, contributed to my growth and resilience.

CHAPTER 2:

BATTLING THE UNCONTROLLABLE

Seizures had cast a profound shadow over my daily life, disrupting my routines and curtailing my engagement in various activities. The impact of these seizures on my life was multifaceted, affecting me physically, mentally, and emotionally. The relentless way they seized control over my moments has meant missing out on crucial school days, leaving an indelible mark on my academic journey.

One of the most unsettling consequences is the toll seizures took on my memory. They swept through my mind like an eraser, leaving me struggling to remember important details and even the simplest tasks. This memory fog further complicated my ability to keep up with schoolwork and retain the knowledge I needed to succeed. The frustration of having my mind betray me was a constant companion, making me feel like I was missing pieces of my life's puzzle.

The physical aftermath of a seizure left me utterly drained as if all the energy had been sapped from my body. The weariness lingered long after the seizure subsided, leaving me exhausted and unable to fully engage in the activities I once enjoyed. Even something as simple as standing up could become a monumental task, as the dizziness that followed a seizure made me feel disoriented and unsteady on my feet. This inability to find my equilibrium left me reliant on support, often forcing me to sit down and catch my breath until the world stopped spinning.

Perhaps the most unsettling aspect of all was the feeling of losing myself. Seizures cast a shadow over my identity, causing me to question who I was when I was not battling against their unpredictable onslaught. The person I knew myself to become a distant figure, obscured by the relentless cycle of seizures and their aftermath.

The impact on my daily activities rippled through every facet of my life. The need for constant vigilance transformed my interactions with others. Family members, particularly my mother, had taken on the role of watchful guardians. The carefree moments of watching friends play or participating in shared activities were no longer a part of my reality. Instead, my mother's watchful eye became my safeguard against the sudden onslaught of a seizure, a reminder of my vulnerability.

Isolation became an unwanted companion as well. The necessity of having someone constantly by my side meant I could never truly be alone. The simple pleasure of solitude, of having time to reflect and recharge, was stripped away by the ever-present need for supervision. The concept of independence took on a new and elusive meaning as I was tethered to the presence of another person, forever linked by the unpredictable nature of my condition.

In the past, I would see many strange things that I couldn't explain. I still remember those times very well. I can remember moments when I felt like I was experiencing something beyond the usual like I was in a place between what was real and what was mysterious. It was like watching a movie of memories playing in front of me.

I often saw strange and unsettling things that felt unreal during a certain time. I remember seeing creatures that looked like demons with horns on their heads. These weird visions appeared in different ways like they were from a scary dream coming to life. This happened a lot to me back then.

I'll never forget one time in my favorite place, the kitchen. As I walked in, something strange happened that I couldn't explain. It felt like everything around me was getting weird and not like how it should be. And at the same time, I started feeling like I was going to have a seizure, which I had experienced before. I was moving into a different way of thinking, and reality didn't seem clear anymore.

At that scary moment, I couldn't believe my eyes. Right there in the kitchen was a strange and scary creature. It had red skin that glowed strangely and horns on its head that made it look even scarier. I felt stuck in a really weird and bad dream as it stared at me. It was like all the badness in the world was focused on me as if trying to challenge me.

I was confused and scared and didn't know what to do. Part of me wanted to run away, but another part of me was curious about what I was seeing. I felt like time had stopped, and I couldn't move because I was scared and interested. The image of that scary thing stayed with me, like a super strong memory that I couldn't forget.

Finally, I woke up fully aware again, escaping the scary dream world. I left the kitchen and the mysterious figure that had confused me. My sense of reality slowly became clearer, but I couldn't forget that strange encounter. It reminded me of the incredible things I had experienced in the past.

Looking back, I've realized that what I saw wasn't like what others saw. Those visions felt very personal, like they came from my complicated thoughts. Even though I saw unbelievable things and felt like I was between two worlds, I now understand that these experiences were special to my journey. They allowed me to see things that were hard to believe – things that felt surreal and out of this world.

I clearly remember feeling so relieved when my seizures finally stopped. It's been a tough journey, but I didn't give up. The last time I had a seizure feels like a distant memory now. I was around thirteen years old back then and dealing with the challenges that epilepsy brought into my life. It's funny how something that used to be a big part of my life is now just something I remember.

When I was a teenager, seizures were always on my mind. They followed me wherever I went, reminding me that I was vulnerable. But then things started to change. I remember the seizures slowly happening less and less. It was like a switch was turned off, and I started to feel more free. Taking my medication every day played a big role in this change. Bit by bit, I felt like I was breaking free from those difficult times.

Looking back on my thirteenth year, it occurred to me that I might have been on the path to recovery for a while before I recognized it. The intervals between seizures grew longer, and their intensity diminished until the day came when they ceased to haunt me altogether. The memory of my last seizure remains a turning point etched into my memory.

Back when I was 16 years old, a significant turning point began to unfold in my life. It marked the moment when I started noticing a remarkable improvement in my health. This change in approach was a game-changer for me. The quality of care I received improved substantially, and with it came a noticeable improvement in my overall well-being. This improvement wasn't solely a matter of fate; it resulted from my commitment to consistently taking my prescribed medication. I diligently stayed up-to-date with my treatment plan, ensuring I never missed a dose. This newfound dedication played a crucial role in my journey toward better health.

Around this time, a pivotal moment arrived when I visited my doctor again. By then, I had followed my treatment regimen meticulously for several months. During this visit, my doctor delivered the news that would further change my life. My Doctor told me I don't need the pills anymore, and I won't have seizures again. From that moment on, I embarked on a journey toward liberation from the shackles of medication.

As fate would have it, life threw some harsh challenges my way. The passing of my mother and the tragic loss of my brother within a span of just a few months cast a shadow over this hopeful period. While grappling with these profound losses, I continued to stay committed to my health journey. Despite the emotional toll these events took on me, I remained steadfast in my determination to persevere.

Over the next few months, as I coped with these personal losses, I returned to the doctor's office. This time, our meeting marked a turning point of a different kind. The doctor's words echoed with certainty – it was time to gradually wean myself off the medication that had been a constant companion for so many years. This step marked a significant milestone in my life. The doctor assured me that the transition would be smooth with their guidance and that I could look forward to a life without the weight of my condition looming over me.

People, indeed, tend to treat you differently when you've gone through such a significant loss. Some family members might act in ways that make you question whether they truly understand your pain. This can manifest as a lack of support or a shift in their interactions with you. It's disheartening when those you expect to be a source of comfort and solace treat you in an aloof or detached manner.

Moreover, certain relatives, like your cousins, might adopt an attitude of detachment. It's as if they believe that they are exempt from the responsibility of offering you genuine support. It's bewildering when you witness your own family members not making an effort to truly be there for you during your times of need. This behavior can leave you feeling isolated and misunderstood.

I understand that the loss of my mother has brought forth a myriad of complex emotions and challenges. It's especially difficult when my cousins, who share a familial bond, distance themselves emotionally. I've learned that some haven't experienced the same loss and might struggle to relate to my feelings. Their lack of understanding may stem from their circumstances.

CHAPTER 3:
FROM TRAGEDY TO
TRANSFORMATION

The passing of my mother, a moment that still echoes in the corridors of my memory, became the most pivotal turning point in my life. In many ways, it felt like a cruel twist of fate, for just when I thought I had conquered the relentless grip of seizures, life threw me into an even darker abyss.

Losing my mother, my anchor in this tumultuous sea of existence, was a blow that shattered my world. She had been my protector, my confidante, and the one person who understood the depths of my struggle with seizures. Losing her meant losing a piece of myself, and it sent shockwaves through the very core of my being.

In the wake of her passing, I was enveloped by a whirlwind of emotions, the most dominant of which was anger. It wasn't just anger at the loss of my mother, but a deep-seated rage at the world for what it had taken from me. This anger became a constant companion, a shadow that followed me through my days and haunted my nights.

The changes that followed my mother's death were profound and far-reaching. I found myself adrift in a world that suddenly seemed cold and unfeeling. The once-familiar routines of life were disrupted, and I struggled to find my footing.

One of the most immediate changes was the impact on my academic life. The emotional turmoil that accompanied my mother's passing made it incredibly difficult to concentrate on my studies. School, which had once been a place of learning and growth, now felt like a battleground for my emotions. My grades plummeted, and I felt a growing distance from my teachers and peers.

But the most significant change was the transformation within me. The anger that had initially consumed me began to evolve into something else—a burning determination to honor my mother's memory by rising above the pain and darkness that had engulfed me. It was a slow and arduous process, but I was determined to reshape my life in a way that would make her proud.

In the aftermath of my mother's passing, I found myself grappling with profound questions about the nature of life and the meaning of my own existence. Why had she been taken from me so soon? Why did I have to endure such pain and loss?

As I sought answers to these questions, I began to look to others who had faced their own tragedies and emerged stronger. I found inspiration in the stories of actors, rappers, and individuals who had overcome their own challenges. These stories became beacons of hope in the darkness, reminding me that it was possible to rise above even the most devastating of circumstances.

I made a decision to channel my anger and grief into productivity. I returned to school, determined to prove to myself that I could succeed despite the odds. I graduated, and then I took a significant step forward by attending Job Corps, a trade school where I learned essential life skills.

Job Corps was a turning point for me. It was there that I gained the practical knowledge and skills I needed to navigate the challenges of adulthood. I obtained my driver's license and graduated with a renewed sense of purpose.

In the end, the passing of my mother, as painful as it was, became the catalyst for my personal transformation. It taught me that life could be unforgiving and unpredictable, but it also showed me that I possessed the inner strength to face adversity head-on. My journey from tragedy to transformation was far from easy, but it was a journey that ultimately led me to a place of newfound strength and understanding.

With each passing day, the anger that had once consumed me began to lose its grip. In its place, I discovered a sense of purpose that I had never known before. My mother's absence was a void that could never be filled, but I realized that I could carry her memory forward in a way that would make her proud.

I immersed myself in activities that resonated with her spirit. I volunteered at a local epilepsy support group, offering my own experiences as a source of encouragement for others battling seizures. It was in these moments of connection and shared pain that I felt a renewed sense of purpose.

The support group also became a lifeline for me. It was a place where I could openly express my grief, anger, and confusion without judgment. Through tears and shared stories, I learned that vulnerability could be a source of strength. I began to understand that it was okay to grieve, to be angry, and to question the unfairness of life. These emotions were part of the healing process, and they didn't diminish the love I had for my mother or the determination to honor her memory.

Returning to school was a challenge, but it was a challenge I willingly embraced. I knew that education was the key to unlocking a brighter future, not just for myself but for the memory of my mother. Every assignment, every exam, and every lecture became a tribute to her unwavering belief in my potential.

As I poured myself into my studies, I found solace in the pursuit of knowledge. The classroom became a sanctuary where I could temporarily escape the weight of my grief and immerse myself in the world of ideas. I discovered a passion for psychology, a subject that allowed me to explore the intricacies of the human mind and the resilience of the human spirit.

In addition to my studies, I turned to another form of therapy—creativity. Writing became an outlet for my emotions, a way to make sense of the turmoil within me. I penned poems that captured the essence of my journey, weaving words into a tapestry of pain, hope, and resilience. It was through these poems that I began to understand the transformative power of art.

I also dabbled in visual arts, creating intricate paintings that expressed the kaleidoscope of emotions swirling within me. Each stroke of the brush was a release, a cathartic process that allowed me to externalize the internal battles I faced.

While my academic pursuits provided a sense of intellectual growth and healing, I knew that practical life skills were equally essential. That realization led me to Job Corps, a place of learning and self-discovery.

Job Corps introduced me to a diverse group of individuals, each with their own stories of triumph over adversity. The camaraderie among us was a balm for our wounded spirits. Together, we learned valuable skills that would equip us for the challenges of adulthood.

I tackled automotive repair, learning the intricacies of engines and transmissions. The grease-stained hands and the smell of motor oil became symbols of my determination to break free from the confines of my past.

Obtaining my driver's license was a milestone I had once thought impossible. The very idea of controlling a vehicle on my own had seemed like an unattainable dream during the darkest days of my seizures. Yet, with unwavering determination and the support of my Job Corps instructors, I achieved this goal.

Driving became a metaphor for my journey from tragedy to transformation. With each mile, I left behind the pain of the past and moved closer to a future filled with promise. It was a tangible reminder that I could conquer the seemingly insurmountable obstacles in my path.

As time passed, the wounds of grief began to heal, though the scars would remain a testament to the love I had for my mother. The anger that had once consumed me evolved into a steely resolve to live a life that would make her proud. I embraced every opportunity to share my story, to inspire others to rise above their own challenges.

In the end, my mother's passing had transformed me in ways I could never have imagined. It had revealed the depths of my own strength and resilience, and it had given me a purpose that transcended my own pain. Through the darkness of tragedy, I had emerged into the light of transformation, carrying with me the memory of the woman who had shaped my life in profound ways.

The passing of my mother had been a crucible of suffering, but it had also been the crucible of my rebirth. It taught me that even in the face of unimaginable loss, we have the power to transform ourselves, to find meaning in the midst of chaos, and to honor the memories of those we love.

My journey from tragedy to transformation was a testament to the indomitable human spirit, a journey marked by resilience, education, creativity, and the unwavering support of those who believed in me. Though I would forever carry the weight of loss, I also carried the torch of hope, lighting the way for others who faced their own dark nights of the soul.

In the end, I had not just survived my mother's passing; I had thrived in her memory, a living tribute to the love and strength she had instilled in me.

CHAPTER 4:

A ROCKY PATH

When I look back at those days, it's hard to believe how much I've changed. Life was a hustle, and I was in the thick of it. The decision to start selling drugs didn't come lightly; it was born out of necessity. I had just completed a grueling thirteen months in Job Corps, a trade school, and I was broke. I needed money, and I needed it fast.

I remember vividly when I decided to start selling drugs. I had two trades under my belt, welding, and carpentry, but jobs in my small town were hard to come by. So, I went to live with my father, hoping to find some stability. It was there that I began my journey into the drug trade.

As I stood at this crossroads of opportunity, I faced a choice that would set me on a path riddled with challenges and self-discovery. My life was about to change in ways I could never have anticipated.

I started small, selling weed. I had a job downtown, working as a housekeeper. It was a way to pay the bills while I dabbled in the world of street sales. At first, it was just a side hustle, a way to make some extra cash. But as I got deeper into it, I realized the potential for profit.

My initiation into the world of street sales was unglamorous. It involved clandestine meetings in dimly lit alleys and exchanges conducted in hushed tones. I had to navigate a subculture that operated on secrecy and codes that were foreign to most.

I never had any moral or ethical conflicts about selling drugs. To me, it was a means of survival. I didn't mind taking care of what I needed to take care of, and I wasn't afraid of the consequences. I needed the money, and I was willing to do what it took to survive.

In the unforgiving landscape of my circumstances, survival was paramount. There was no room for hesitation or doubt. My focus shifted from the conventional ideals of right and wrong to the raw necessity of existence. The drug trade was my lifeline, and I clung to it tightly.

There were no influential people pushing me into the drug trade. I was my own influencer. I knew I had to make money, and I took it upon myself to do so. I started carrying a small gun, a .22, for protection. It was a tough world out there, and I had to watch my back.

As a lone wolf in this perilous endeavor, my instincts became my guiding light. I learned to trust no one but myself, relying on intuition to navigate the murky waters of the drug trade. The small firearm I carried was a constant reminder of the dangers that lurked in the shadows, a necessary evil in a world where self-preservation was paramount.

As I got deeper into selling drugs, my personality began to change. I became meaner and more focused on my own needs. I didn't care about anyone else; I was just trying to make ends meet. I worked a job and sold weed, all while packing my little .22 with me everywhere I went.

The transformation was gradual but undeniable. The relentless pursuit of profit hardened my demeanor. The world I inhabited was unforgiving, and I had to adapt to survive. Empathy became a luxury I couldn't afford, and my once amiable disposition gave way to a more guarded and ruthless persona.

There were no warning signs for me during this time. I was always cautious and kept a close eye on the people I was dealing with. I didn't trust anyone fully, and I made sure to have my gun ready in case things went south. It was a risky business, and I knew it.

Every transaction, every encounter, was a potential minefield. My survival depended on constant vigilance. Trust was a scarce commodity, and I had to tread carefully. The specter of danger loomed over me, a constant reminder of the perils of my chosen path.

Selling drugs didn't have a significant impact on my family or close friends. In fact, some of them bought weed from me. My cousin, nephews, and even my brother purchased from me. I'd sell to my friends, and they'd sometimes hook me up with other people who wanted to buy. It was a tight-knit circle, and it worked for us.

Within the cocoon of my social circle, the dynamics of our relationships remained intact. The drug trade was just another facet of our lives, a shared secret that bound us closer. It was a paradoxical existence, as the illegal trade coexisted with the familiarity of family and friends.

There weren't many incidents or confrontations directly related to my drug dealing. Most of the trouble I found was due to personal conflicts and arguments, not the business itself.

Walking the razor's edge between legality and criminality, I had to be vigilant not to let the two worlds collide. It was the personal skirmishes that posed the greatest threat to my newfound livelihood. The line between my business and my private life became increasingly blurred, and I had to be cautious not to let it all come crashing down.

I was lucky not to face legal consequences for selling drugs. My legal troubles were related to the altercations I had with people I got into arguments with. There was one incident where I beat someone with my gun during a heated dispute. The police were called, and I ended up behind bars.

My luck, however, was not boundless. The incident that led to my arrest served as a stark reminder of the precipice I teetered on. The consequences of my actions were never far from my thoughts, and the specter of imprisonment loomed ever closer.

My time in jail wasn't pleasant. I was handcuffed to the person I had beaten with my gun, and it was a tense situation. He eventually got sent back to Mississippi due to previous legal issues, and I managed to get my charges dropped.

Jail was a sobering experience, a stark contrast to the chaotic world I had left behind. The cold, unforgiving bars and the ever-present sense of confinement were a harsh wake-up call. It was in this desolate environment that I caught a glimpse into the abyss, realizing the fragility of my freedom.

During those days, I didn't have any remorse for my actions. I was wild and carefree, focused on making money, selling weed, and enjoying my life. I had no feelings or moral qualms; I was addicted to the hustle.

My existence was unapologetic, a life unburdened by guilt or regret. I had become a creature of the shadows, driven by a relentless pursuit of financial gain. The moral compass I once possessed had been temporarily silenced by the cacophony of my daily struggles.

Despite my legal issues, I never got caught selling drugs. I was meticulous in my dealings and had a strategy to minimize risks. I made sure to only deal with people I knew or got to know. They'd come to my car for transactions, and I never let anyone sit behind me, always in the front passenger seat for my safety.

My life was a complex dance of evasion and discretion. I honed the art of subterfuge, ensuring that I remained one step ahead of the authorities. Every detail, from the choice of clientele to the location of transactions, was a calculated move in the intricate game I played.

I did have plans for my future, even though I was deeply involved in the drug trade. I knew that I couldn't sell drugs forever. So, I worked a job while still selling weed on the side. My goal was to stack as much money as I could, with the hope that one day, I could transition away from the drug trade.

My determination to secure a future beyond the drug trade was an undercurrent beneath the chaos of my present existence. I recognized the transient nature of my illicit endeavors and sought to accumulate resources that would pave the way for a different life. It was a delicate balance, the tension between immediate gain and a distant dream.

As time went on, I eventually did stop selling weed after seventeen and a half years in the game. I got two jobs, continuing to work hard and save money. It was time for a change, but I couldn't imagine a life without a little weed to relax.

The transition away from the drug trade marked the end of an era. It was a bittersweet farewell to a life I had known for nearly two decades. The decision to abandon my illicit trade was a testament to my resilience and determination to seek a better future. The lure of a more conventional life beckoned, and I embraced the opportunity for change.

Life during those days was a hustle, but it was my hustle. It was a chapter of my life that I'll never forget, a period of survival, risk, and reward. Looking back, it's incredible to see how far I've come and how much I've changed. The drug trade was a part of my past, but it doesn't define me.

In retrospect, those tumultuous years served as a crucible that forged the person I would become. They were a testament to my resilience, resourcefulness, and adaptability. The drug trade, once a means of survival, now stands as a chapter in my life story, a testament to the transformative power of determination and the human spirit.

Life after the drug trade brought its own set of challenges and opportunities. I found myself at a crossroads once again, but this time the path was one of redemption and rebuilding. The experiences and lessons I had gained during my time in the shadows would prove invaluable in the journey that lay ahead.

My story is not one of glorification but of reflection and growth. The drug trade was a chapter, but it was not the whole story. It was a journey through the depths of adversity, and it tested the limits of my resolve. In its aftermath, I emerged a changed person, carrying with me the wisdom and scars of my past.

I often think back to those days when I was immersed in the hustle, and it's hard to believe how much I've changed. The shadows of my past continue to linger, but they no longer define me. My life has evolved, and I am no longer the person I once was.

The decision to sell drugs, born out of necessity, was a turning point in my life. It set me on a path filled with challenges and uncertainties. It was a journey through the shadows, where survival was the primary goal.

As I look back at those days, I am reminded of the person I once was and the person I have become. The drug trade was a chapter in my life, a chapter that tested my mettle, reshaped my character, and ultimately led me to a different path.

My transformation from a street seller of drugs to a person who sought stability and a brighter future was not easy. It required a significant shift in mindset, a departure from the ruthless world of street sales to a life of conventional work and lawful living.

The drug trade was never a choice made lightly. It was a response to the pressing need for money and survival. With two trades under my belt, I had hoped to secure a stable job, but the harsh reality of a small town with limited opportunities led me down a different road.

In the early days, my foray into the world of street sales was tentative. I sold weed while working as a housekeeper downtown, using it as a means to make ends meet. The world I entered was shrouded in secrecy and shadow, a subculture with its own codes and customs.

My moral compass had to adapt to the harsh realities of survival. Selling drugs was a means to an end, a way to secure my own well-being. It was not a decision made lightly, but it was a path I was willing to walk.

The drug trade was not imposed upon me by influential figures. I was my own influencer, driven by the urgency of my circumstances. To survive, I embraced a life that required constant vigilance, carrying a small .22 for protection and navigating a world fraught with risks.

The transformation I underwent was both internal and external. I became hardened, meaner, and more focused on my own needs. The hustle became an addiction, a way of life that left no room for compassion or hesitation. Survival in this world demanded a relentless pursuit of personal gain.

Throughout my journey, there were no clear warning signs. I operated with caution, a watchful eye on those I interacted with. Trust was a rare commodity, and I was always prepared for the unexpected. The small .22 I carried was a constant reminder of the precarious nature of my existence.

My journey through the drug trade had a limited impact on my family and close friends. In fact, some of them became customers, blurring the lines between my personal life and my illicit business. It was a tight-knit circle, one that provided a sense of security in the otherwise tumultuous world I inhabited.

While there were occasional confrontations, most of the trouble I encountered was a result of personal disputes rather than the drug trade itself. The line between my business and my personal life was thin, and I had to be cautious not to let them intersect.

Legal troubles did loom over me, but they were not directly tied to my drug dealings. Instead, it was a violent altercation that led to my arrest. I found myself behind bars, a place where the harsh realities of my actions were inescapable. It was a stark reminder of the consequences that could befall me.

During my time in jail, I was confronted with the weight of my actions. Handcuffed to the person I had harmed, the tension was palpable. My future hung in the balance, and I had to grapple with the reality of my choices.

Despite my legal troubles, I harbored no remorse for my actions. I was consumed by the hustle, intoxicated by the fast-paced world of street sales. Morality had become a distant memory, overshadowed by the need to survive.

In my pursuit of financial gain, I maintained a careful balance, avoiding legal consequences for my drug dealings. My meticulous approach minimized the risks, and I only dealt with those I knew or had come to trust. Transactions took place in my car, with strict precautions to ensure my safety. As time passed, I began to contemplate a future beyond the drug trade. I recognized that my involvement in this illicit world could not be sustained indefinitely. To transition away from it, I held down a job while continuing to sell weed on the side. The goal was to accumulate as much capital as possible, paving the way for a different life in the future.

My resolve to build a more stable life would lead to the eventual cessation of my involvement in the drug trade. After 17 and a half years in the game, I made the difficult decision to step away. It was a significant turning point, marked by the pursuit of two legitimate jobs and a steadfast commitment to saving money.

The transition from a life immersed in the hustle of drug sales to a more conventional existence was not without its challenges. It required a complete transformation in the way I approached life, work, and personal relationships. The drug trade, once the dominant force in my life, slowly began to recede into the past.

Looking back, those days were a tumultuous chapter in my life, characterized by survival, risk, and reward. It was a period marked by resilience, resourcefulness, and adaptation. The drug trade, though it once defined me, no longer held that power. It had become a part of my history, a testament to the transformative capacity of the human spirit.

Life after the drug trade brought its own set of challenges and opportunities. I found myself at a crossroads once again, but this time the path was one of redemption and rebuilding. The experiences and lessons I had gained during my time in the shadows would prove invaluable in the journey that lay ahead.

In the years that followed, I continued to reflect on the person I had once been and the person I had become. The drug trade was a pivotal chapter in my life, a chapter that tested my mettle, reshaped my character, and ultimately led me to a different path.

My story is not one of glorification but of reflection and growth. It's a testament to the transformative power of determination and resilience. The drug trade, once a means of survival, now stands as a chapter in my life story, a chapter that I've learned from, but one that does not define me.

CHAPTER 5:

DANCE OF FATE

Life felt like a winding road with twists and turns, leading me through a series of challenges that seemed insurmountable. My run-ins with the law, like repeating chapters in a book I couldn't put down, became increasingly serious. Seven times I found myself behind bars, each release accompanied by a warning that the next stint might land me in prison.

Jail, a cold and unforgiving place, became a temporary home where time seemed to crawl. During a two-week stretch, I found myself in a state of apathy. I didn't care about anything, and others stayed away, sensing the darkness within me. It was a lonely period, where I became someone even I didn't want to be.

Evil, they labeled me. People kept their distance, conversations were scarce, and my cell became a solitary haven for a malevolent presence. It was a harsh realization of the person I had become, and the reflection in the steel mirror painted a grim picture.

To avoid the looming threat of prison, the legal system directed me to a place called CCC. Daytime hours were spent locked up, and I was granted freedom to work outside. It was a routine, a conditional liberty where each step I took was monitored, and the fear of prison lingered like a ghost in the shadows.

The legal system became a strict guide, leading me through a carefully choreographed routine. The steps involved navigating the complexities of parole, court appearances, and legal strategies. Each move had consequences, and the dance with the law became a delicate balancing act between maintaining freedom and avoiding the clutches of prison.

This legal routine wasn't just a physical exercise; it became a deep philosophical exploration. It made me ponder not only the legal intricacies but the broader implications of my choices. The stage upon which I performed became a microcosm of the larger world, reflecting the consequences of my past actions and the responsibility I bore for my destiny.

In the solitude of this legal journey, moments of reflection were profound. I thought not only about legal intricacies but also about personal responsibility. The dance with fate became a mirror reflecting the consequences of my past actions and the responsibility I bore for my own destiny.

The legal system, like a strict instructor, demanded discipline and adherence to a prescribed routine. I became a student in the art of navigating the legal labyrinth, a dancer whose survival depended on mastering the intricate movements of the judicial ballet. The dance of legality was both a test and a lesson, a crucible in which I forged a renewed sense of personal responsibility.

As I moved through the routine of conditional freedom, the philosophical underpinnings of my journey began to crystallize. The stage upon which I moved became a metaphor for the transformative power of personal responsibility. Each step, each decision, was a brushstroke on the canvas of my redemption.

The legal intricacies, once perceived as barriers, became the very steps that led me to a profound understanding of personal responsibility. The legal system, initially seen as an adversary, became a partner in my journey of rehabilitation and renewal. It was not just a dance with the law but a dance with self, a reflection on the consequences of my choices and the responsibility I bore for my destiny.

As the curtain fell on this chapter of my life, I carried with me the wisdom gleaned from this journey. The legal routine had not only changed my legal status but had orchestrated a metamorphosis of the soul. I emerged not as a prisoner of my past but as someone who had learned the value of responsibility, navigating through the shadows and emerging into a new phase of life defined by choices, consequences, and the enduring journey with fate.

CHAPTER 6:

TRIUMPH IN ADVERSITY

Life is an enigmatic voyage, a series of challenges intricately woven into the fabric of our existence. For me, these trials weren't mere hurdles but rather passages demanding transformation, each a compelling narrative of resilience sculpted through adversity.

Among the most profound challenges I encountered was the realization that certain facets of my life were counteractive to my growth. It necessitated a painful but vital choice: to disengage from circles that didn't resonate with my aspirations. This pivotal shift propelled me toward embracing positive influences, gravitating towards relationships and environments that resonated with my ambitions.

Resilience, a relentless pursuit, often demands a solo odyssey in the absence of a guiding mentor. It meant charting a solitary course, sifting through life's turbulent moments to extract fragments of positivity, and transforming every setback into a catalyst for personal growth.

In the depths of contemplation, stories became a refuge—particularly documentaries. These cinematic narratives offered profound insights into the lives of those who confronted and conquered tribulations, much like the saga of Ice-T. Their tales served as luminous beacons, illuminating the possibility of navigating the labyrinthine corridors of adversity.

Fostering and preserving a positive mindset necessitated a scrupulous examination of my surroundings. It meant curating environments that fostered optimism, ensuring my inner sanctum comprised genuine and supportive souls. This nurturing ecosystem emerged as a powerful catalyst in shaping my worldview and approach toward life's daunting tests.

Amidst the tempests of existence, I discovered the art of preserving composure amidst the whirlwind of stress. Strolls through familiar alleys or scenic drives became avenues for unfettered contemplation, offering vistas for strategic thought and novel perspectives from interactions with kindred spirits.

The weight of stress often found its release in intimate connections. Engaging with companions provided not just solace but a reorientation of thoughts, rendering me better equipped to confront the challenges that loomed ahead.

The impact of surmounting these trials rippled beyond my own existence, resonating deeply within my sphere. Friends who bore witness to my journey found inspiration in my resilience. Conversations veered towards collective improvement, forging a common quest for enhanced lives.

Through these defining crucibles, the sanctity of positive routines was revealed. Exercise, transcending the realm of physicality, became a sanctuary to fortify both physique and psyche, rendering not just strength but also clarity and motivation. Establishing routines that granted moments of respite and mental lucidity emerged as foundational pillars of my resilience.

Each stratagem I adopted was an unrelenting endeavor to sustain an unshakeable optimism. The chronicles of others' triumphs became a guiding light, catalyzing the reshaping of my existence for the better. It wasn't solely about overcoming hurdles; it was about evolving into an exemplar, instilling in those around me an aspiration for continual growth, and embracing the profound resilience inherent within the human spirit.

CHAPTER 7:
REDEFINING IDENTITY

Identity, akin to a vibrant mosaic, intricately fashions itself from the amalgamation of our experiences, beliefs, and interactions with the world. It is a canvas painted with the diverse hues of life's encounters, each stroke shaping the vivid picture of our existence. These moments, whether exuberant or melancholic, etch themselves onto this canvas, forming the rich foundation upon which our sense of self blossoms.

Our beliefs act as the scaffolding of this evolving mosaic, grounding our values and convictions into the very essence of our being. Like the vivid pigments in an artist's palette, these beliefs infuse the canvas with depth and meaning, dictating the colors that define our worldview and decisions.

Moreover, our reactions to life's challenges serve as the sculptor's chisel, etching new lines and contours onto this living masterpiece. How we respond to adversity, embrace triumphs, and navigate the complexities of our journey, each contribute to the ever-expanding mosaic of our identity. Every choice, every action, becomes a tessera carefully set into place, intricately interlocking with the existing mosaic, continuously shaping and redefining the landscape of our identity.

This mosaic of identity is an evolving portrait, a living narrative within us. It is not stagnant but fluid, a testament to our growth and evolution. With each passing moment, new fragments are added, enriching the complexity of this vibrant composition that narrates the story of who we are. Much like an artist constantly adding layers of meaning to their canvas, our identity, too, is a mosaic that continually adapts, portraying the intricate beauty of our lived experiences.

In the intricate labyrinth of my recollections, certain moments emerge as luminescent beacons, illuminating the path towards an unfiltered truth. These are the instances where the meticulously crafted facades of individuals, meticulously maintained shields meant to conceal vulnerabilities, cracked and crumbled, revealing the raw and unvarnished authenticity within. These rare unveilings, akin to discovering hidden treasures within the depths of the mundane, held an inexplicable allure, imprinting themselves deeply upon the canvas of my consciousness.

These moments weren't merely glimpses into someone else's truth; they were revelations that echoed the sanctity of honesty. It was in these instances that the profound beauty of authenticity shone through, transcending the veil of societal norms and pretense. Witnessing the unguarded soul beneath the layers of presentation served as an indelible reminder of the authenticity I sought not only in others but also within myself.

In the quiet aftermath of these revelations, a profound realization took root: authenticity, this unadulterated expression of self, is the bedrock upon which genuine connections are forged. It became evident that these rare unveilings weren't just about the individuals themselves; they symbolized a larger truth about human connections. Authenticity, much like the resonating notes of a harmonious melody, creates an atmosphere where trust, intimacy, and understanding thrive effortlessly.

Conversely, the absence of truth, the dissonance that arises from pretense and deceit, casts a pall over the symphony of connections. It alters the hues and tones through which relationships are perceived, distorting the lens through which I view the world. Like a discordant note in an otherwise melodious composition, the absence of authenticity disrupts the harmony of interactions, leaving an imprint that reverberates far beyond the initial encounter.

These pivotal moments became guiding stars in navigating the landscape of my relationships. They instilled in me an unwavering commitment to seek authenticity in every interaction, to foster spaces where genuineness could flourish without fear of judgment or rejection. They illuminated the understanding that genuine connections aren't merely forged through shared experiences or commonalities; they are rooted in the honesty of expression and the willingness to embrace vulnerability.

The resonance of these moments extended beyond mere interpersonal relationships; they became fundamental in shaping the prism through which I perceive the world. They reinforced the importance of seeking truth in all its forms, of cherishing the genuine over the manufactured, and of embracing authenticity as a guiding principle in navigating the complexities of human interactions.

Thus, these instances of raw authenticity served as transformative catalysts, altering not just my perception of others but also laying the groundwork for a deeper understanding of myself. They remain as enduring reminders of the profound beauty encapsulated within the simplicity of honesty, reminding me that within every human soul lies a treasure trove of authenticity waiting to be discovered and cherished.

My odyssey of self-discovery unfolded as a solitary pilgrimage into the depths of my being, a deliberate endeavor to sculpt the very essence of my existence without the looming specter of external influences. This deliberate pursuit of self-realization was a deliberate departure from the norms and societal pressures that often dictate the paths we tread, granting me the liberty to embark on an unencumbered exploration of the recesses of my identity.

Solitude emerged as my steadfast companion on this inward expedition, offering a refuge where the clamor of the external world dissipated, allowing the symphony of my innermost thoughts and emotions to resound. Amidst this tranquility, I engaged in a profound dialogue with the echo chambers of my soul, a conversation that beckoned me to do more than merely listen—it implored me to truly hear, to grasp the murmurs and echoes that resonated from the core of my being.

The societal frameworks that envelop our lives attempted to weave their intricate webs around my identity, aiming to ensnare me within their predefined molds. However, resolute in my determination to chart a path guided by my truth, I adamantly resisted succumbing to the gravitational pull of societal expectations. These constructs, foreign to the melody of my essence, failed to dictate the narrative of my journey.

Inevitably, clashes arose as my self-perception collided headlong with the expectations imposed upon me by others. Yet, anchored firmly in the bastion of authenticity, I remained steadfast, refusing to dilute the purity of my essence for the mere sake of conforming to the comfort zones of others.

The reconciliation I pursued was an introspective endeavor—an internal sanctuary where the alignment of my instincts, values, and beliefs became the cornerstone of my existence. Trusting these guiding principles offered solace— a sanctuary in the authenticity I fiercely upheld, a sanctuary that shielded me from the incessant pressures seeking to mold and reshape my identity to fit predefined molds.

This internal harmony was a refuge, a sanctuary where the authenticity I nurtured was not a product of compromise but a testament to the unwavering commitment to remain true to the essence of who I am. It was a conscious embrace of my individuality, an acknowledgment that the resonance of my identity need not bend to the winds of external influence but stand tall as an unwavering testament to my truth.

The transformative shift in my perception of trust was a seismic recalibration, a profound realization that trust, akin to a delicate glass sculpture, must be meticulously crafted and earned rather than naively bestowed. Recognizing its fragility, I navigated the terrain of relationships with a discerning eye, allowing only the most genuine connections to breach the fortified walls guarding my trust. Each interaction became a delicate dance, a measured evaluation of intentions and actions, fostering an environment where authenticity and sincerity were the linchpins of trust.

Simultaneously, my measure of success underwent a profound metamorphosis, transcending the superficiality of external validation to embrace the sanctum of inner contentment. The pursuit of fulfillment ceased to be a pursuit of accolades or external affirmations; instead, it became a pilgrimage toward authenticity, a journey that involved nurturing the flames of my passions and plumbing the unfathomable depths of self-understanding before attempting to decipher the complexities of the world around me.

The crucible of betrayal, a furnace that seared through trust and relationships, yielded invaluable lessons. It wasn't merely a scar but an epiphany—a catalyst that fortified my resolve to stay anchored in the authenticity of my being, impervious to the tempests seeking to sway me from my truth. It was an acknowledgment that while betrayal might wound, it couldn't diminish the authenticity I ardently preserved.

My identity underwent a profound transformation, evolving into a guiding beacon that illuminated my interactions and relationships. Personally, it fostered deeper connections steeped in authenticity, where vulnerability was embraced and trust was nurtured. Professionally, it infused collaborations and interactions with an aura of trust and sincerity, fostering an environment conducive to genuine growth and understanding.

The fervor for competition, for me, transcended the mere pursuit of victory. It wasn't about besting others but about an unwavering quest for self-improvement. It fueled the fire of my ambition, an intrinsic facet of my identity that propelled relentless strides toward personal growth, constantly pushing boundaries and reaching for higher planes of self-realization.

Redefining identity wasn't an event etched in stone but an ongoing evolution, a mosaic woven from the threads of experiences and introspection. Each experience, each profound moment of self-reflection, contributed its vibrant brushstroke to the intricate canvas that envelops the very fabric of my being. This journey persists, for identity, akin to the undulating rhythm of life itself, remains an unceasing state of becoming—an ever-unfolding narrative of self-discovery and growth, a testament to the resilience and fluidity of the human spirit.

CHAPTER 8:

BUILDING A NEW LIFE

In the quiet moments, surrounded by humble cushions, I found myself retracing the steps of my life—a story of rebuilding, resilience, and rediscovery.

There emerged pivotal moments that illuminated the path toward a more stable future. It was a conscious decision—to plunge back into the world of medical coding and billing. The resonance of that choice echoed through the corridors of time, not merely as lessons from online courses in 2008 and 2009 but as deliberate steps paving the way toward a brighter tomorrow.

Amid the complexities of my troubled history, the decision to reenter the realm of medical coding and billing stood out as a beacon of hope. Those online courses weren't just about acquiring knowledge; they represented a profound commitment to self-improvement and a resilient resolve to forge a steadier path ahead. Each module became a stepping stone, building a foundation for a future characterized by stability and purpose.

Life's obstacles weren't merely external challenges; some found their roots within me. The journey of redefining my identity wasn't a mere rearrangement of career pieces; it was a profound metamorphosis. It extended beyond the surface, representing a deliberate shift in my attitudes and behaviors.

Amid the external roadblocks, there existed internal struggles that demanded attention. The quest to redefine who I was became an inward exploration, a journey into the recesses of my own thoughts and emotions. It was more than adapting to a new career; it was a conscious evolution of self—a transformative process that required me to scrutinize my beliefs, adjust my attitudes, and reshape the very core of who I was.

The professional expedition unfolded as a canvas, and on it, I painted strokes of fulfillment. In this realm, pleasing oneself wasn't a selfish pursuit; it became an indispensable necessity. The narrative wasn't confined to the confines of work; it transcended into finding joy in the cadence of daily tasks—a harmonious melody of success.

Every step in the professional journey wasn't just a means to an end; it became a stroke on the canvas of personal fulfillment. Pleasing oneself emerged as the key to unlocking a richer, more satisfying professional existence. It wasn't about selfish desires but a recognition that true success resonates from within, creating a symphony of contentment amid the daily grind.

Beyond the mundane routines of work, there lay a deeper understanding—that professional success isn't solely measured by external accolades but by the internal harmony one achieves. The melody of success wasn't a grand crescendo but a series of harmonious notes played in the everyday rhythm of tasks and accomplishments, each contributing to the masterpiece of a fulfilled professional journey.

Personal pursuits and connections assumed center stage—a four-year voyage marked by mutual support and shared dreams. The genesis of a website wasn't merely an exhibition of digital prowess; it emerged as a symbol of collaboration and shared aspirations.

The four-year journey wasn't a solitary venture but a shared odyssey, characterized by mutual encouragement and the weaving together of dreams. Personal endeavors, entwined with relationships, became a narrative that transcended the individual. Within this shared timeline, the creation of a website served as a tangible emblem—a testament not only to technical skills but, more importantly, to the power of collaboration and collective aspirations.

The website's significance echoed beyond the virtual realm, resonating with the spirit of joint ventures and combined efforts. It wasn't just about crafting a digital presence; it symbolized the strength found in unity, a reminder that even in personal pursuits, the support and collaboration of others can transform individual dreams into shared victories.

In the relentless pursuit of self-discovery and growth, I find myself standing before the mirror, examining the very essence of who I am. This introspection is not merely a glance; it is a deliberate effort to unearth the best within me. The journey unfolds not only as an exploration but as a conscious decision to bring out the most positive aspects of my identity.

To grow, I believe in cultivating a mindset that constantly seeks improvement. Looking at myself in the mirror becomes a ritual, a moment of self-reflection where I identify strengths that can be amplified. It's about embracing the elements that make me unique and leveraging them to foster personal happiness and development.

One key element of this ongoing journey is the commitment to maintaining a positive attitude. I am determined to uplift myself, to exude confidence that reverberates in everything I do. Speaking positively about myself, avoiding self-deprecation, and always holding my head high contribute to a mindset that fuels growth.

Personal care is another crucial facet of this process. Ensuring that I present the best version of myself externally, from clean clothes to well-ironed attire, is part of the holistic approach to growth. It symbolizes a commitment to self-respect and an acknowledgment that my external presentation influences my internal well-being.

Beyond appearances, my financial and personal independence play pivotal roles in this journey. Having the means to explore, move, and engage in various activities enhances my sense of self. It allows me to make decisions based on personal desires and aspirations, contributing significantly to my overall growth.

In the complex network of relationships, vulnerability becomes a crucial thread, weaving authenticity into the fabric of connection. Instances arise where one must open up, exposing one's true self, yet maintaining a delicate balance to shield against potential harm.

Reflecting on personal experiences, there have been moments when vulnerability played a pivotal role in fostering authenticity within my relationships. It is an acknowledgment that I am human, with emotions and vulnerabilities that make me authentic. However, striking the right balance between openness and protecting oneself is a delicate dance.

When faced with potential harm within a relationship, my approach is multifaceted. Firstly, I distance myself from those causing harm. Recognizing toxicity or harm, I make a conscious decision to step away, creating a physical and emotional space between us. This serves as a protective measure, preventing further damage.

Secondly, I choose not to engage with such individuals anymore. Cutting ties is not a sign of weakness; rather, it is a display of strength and self-preservation. By removing them from my life, I eliminate the avenues through which harm could manifest.

The third step involves a mental shift. I consciously forget about their presence, as if they were never a part of my life. This mental closure is crucial for my own well-being and growth. It allows me to move forward without the weight of past negative experiences dragging me down.

Moving on with life is the final and most crucial step. This means not only physically distancing myself but also emotionally detaching. I cease all contact – no calls, no messages. If they attempt to reach out, I block their number. This intentional disconnection is a powerful statement that I will not allow harm into my life.

Expectations in relationships, whether personal or professional, play a significant role in this dynamic. While it is natural to expect reciprocity when we extend goodness, it is essential to navigate these expectations with a level-headed approach. Expectations, if left unchecked, can lead to disappointments and unmet needs.

However, expectations can be managed through open communication. Honest conversations about needs, desires, and boundaries help set realistic expectations. Mutual understanding fosters healthier relationships where both parties feel heard and respected.

n my journey, maintaining authenticity amidst external pressures and potential harm has been crucial. I believe that letting negativity and harm persist allows it to escalate, and it's essential to prioritize self-preservation. Trusting others can be risky, as relationships can turn from friendship to enmity unexpectedly. It's a reminder that one must be cautious and not let anyone bring harm.

Expectations, too, can be a source of potential harm, especially when we don't receive something positive in return. Allowing others to have authority over us without reciprocal benefits can lead to detrimental consequences. It's a lesson in setting boundaries and being mindful of the potential harm we might encounter.

Reflecting on authenticity and dealing with external pressures, I've found that staying true to myself is paramount. Social expectations can be challenging to navigate, but prioritizing personal happiness and peace is vital. It's crucial to remember that oneself comes first in the face of criticism and negativity. Prioritizing one's well-being and staying motivated can help combat external pressures.

Regarding the intersection between internal harmony and external influences, socializing can be both rewarding and challenging. Dealing with different personalities across personal, social, and professional spheres requires understanding and adapting. It's essential to engage with the right people who contribute positively to one's life and avoid those who bring negativity.

In my journey, role models like Ice T have played a significant role. Ice T's life story, from adversity to success, resonates with me. His ability to overcome challenges and stay motivated inspires me to keep going. During tough times, the stories and motivational speeches of role models can serve as a guiding light, providing strength and encouragement.

While some may argue that motivational speeches may seem vague during tough times, I find solace and motivation in the experiences of my role models. Ice T's journey from adversity to success reminds me that challenges can be overcome with a positive mindset. Having a role model like him has been instrumental in shaping my personal and professional growth.

Reflecting on the role of self-reflection and introspection in my life, I consider decision-making a crucial aspect. Making the right decisions is imperative, as a wrong choice can have severe consequences. I believe in thinking about a decision thoroughly, often five to ten times, considering the pros and cons, potential outcomes, and the impact on my life.

I prioritize making rational and practical decisions, avoiding impulsivity. This involves a comprehensive thought process, including brainstorming and asking WH questions (who, what, how, when, where). I weigh the consequences and benefits, ensuring that the decision aligns with my long-term goals and well-being.

This practice of introspection and careful decision-making has been vital in guiding me through life. It's a strategy to come out as a winner, avoiding potential pitfalls that impulsive decisions might lead to.

Setbacks and doubts, I discovered, were not detours but integral chapters of the journey. The crucial lesson became not to dwell in stagnation but to persistently move forward. The essence lay in preserving a positive outlook—a straightforward yet formidable strategy to navigate the storms that life hurled my way.

In the complex narrative of life, setbacks weren't barriers but rather twists in the plot, and doubts weren't deterrents but elements that added depth to the storyline. The essential realization was that progress wasn't defined by the absence of challenges but by the unwavering commitment to surmount them. Moving forward wasn't a mere action; it was a mindset—a conscious choice to keep striding ahead despite the hurdles.

The wisdom accrued from this chapter wasn't about avoiding the storms but about learning to dance in the rain. The key wasn't to eliminate setbacks but to transform them into stepping stones. Holding onto a positive outlook wasn't just a coping mechanism; it emerged as a beacon, guiding the way through the darkest moments, a testament to the resilience embedded in the simplicity of optimism.

The definition of success underwent a quiet revolution. It wasn't about external validations but an internal compass. "I believe in myself," became the anthem—a reminder that self-belief often outweighs external opinions.

Betrayal cast shadows, and yet, amid the disappointment, unconventional coping mechanisms emerged. Bars and casinos became spaces of escape and strategy, places to plan a resilient comeback.

CHAPTER 9:
INSPIRING OTHERS

I hope that my story can motivate and give hope to those who hear it. Going from nothing to success has not been an easy journey, but if sharing my experiences can inspire even one other person, it makes all the struggles worth it.

Throughout my childhood and teenage years, I faced immense challenges. Living with epilepsy and seizures disrupted my life in many ways. The losses of my mother and brother left deep wounds that took a long time to heal. There were so many nights where I didn't think I could go on, but something inside drove me to keep fighting. If my story shows others that perseverance is possible even in the darkest of times, then all the hardships were not in vain.

My goal has never been to dwell on past hardships, but to use them to help empower others. I want people to understand that our circumstances do not determine our potential. Through diligent effort and community support, we all have the strength to overcome obstacles and create positive change in our lives. At different points in my journey, caring individuals extended a helping hand that gave me the courage to keep going. I hope hearing how others contributed to my success inspires listeners to offer support within their own communities.

Today, I strive to "break the cycle of mediocrity through dignified work." By providing jobs, training programs and reinvesting profits at the Center for Men, I aim to demonstrate that stable careers are accessible regardless of one's past. I want current and former residents to see that their situation today does not have to dictate their future if given the right opportunities and resources. Through my businesses, I hope others find the courage to believe in themselves as I have.

Beyond publishing my story in written form, I try to share my experiences directly as much as possible. Speaking at shelters, community centers and schools allows me a chance to interact with audiences and answer questions. I find great reward in listening to individuals share how my words or guidance have resonated with them. It is an honor to be seen as a positive role model and source of inspiration by members of Milwaukee. If my visibility in the community motivates even one person the way others once motivated me, it makes the effort worthwhile.

On a broader scale, I strive to inspire collective efforts that protect vulnerable populations. Holding leadership roles with charities and in local government allows me a platform to advocate for causes close to my heart. I aim to educate others on the challenges facing at-risk groups through sharing insights from my own experiences navigating hardships. If collectively we can develop more compassion for socio-economically disadvantaged communities and implement supportive policies, it will enhance well-being for many.

Once I complete writing this memoir, profits from sales will fund my lifelong dream of establishing another shelter facility. There, through my expanded model of rehabilitation services integrated with job training programs, I hope to empower even more people to turn their lives around. If expanding the shelter can lift hundreds from hardship as the initial one lifted me, it will be the highest honor. I hope that showing others how opportunity rescued me will motivate communities everywhere to practice compassion and dedicate resources toward preventing and ending hardships.

I hope that sharing my story can inspire and motivate others in meaningful ways. Looking back on overcoming immense hardships throughout my childhood and teenage years, I strive to portray the power of perseverance when facing difficulties. Despite enduring challenges with epilepsy, losses of my mother and brother, I refused to surrender to my circumstances. By staying committed to managing my health even amid emotional turmoil, as detailed in prior chapters, I aim to showcase how prioritizing one's wellbeing can aid overcoming life's darkest times. Others may lose hope, but I want to inspire viewing each day as an opportunity to progress rather than dwell in past suffering. Recalling old wounds only postpones new growth, as I've realized clinging to anger and grief solely hinders moving forward.

My journey aims sparking hope that no challenge need define a person if equipped with determination and backing systems. Through caring individuals empowering me during seizures, I found strength to fight on alone. My path emphasizes community support uplifting vulnerable communities instead of leaving them to fend entirely for themselves. By finishing trade training despite epilepsy disrupting memory, I hope to reassure others their circumstances do not dictate capabilities. With diligence and proper resources, stable careers remain accessible regardless of past ups and downs.

I candidly recount witnessing a friend's death at age 14 to shed light on dark subjects seldom voiced. By breaking taboos surrounding such realities, I aim fostering understanding for those navigating similarly harsh circumstances in underprivileged areas. Detailing my transformation from street sales out of necessity into establishing thriving enterprises uplifts spirits knowing others climbed from rock bottom, too. My success signals struggling individuals' present troubles need not define lifelong prospects with optimism and community backing. The empowerment I and my organization bring former residents signals supportive paths leading to dignified futures.

Recent Midwest talks focus sparking collective action through storytelling. By discussing issues exacerbating hardships and advocating pragmatic policy discussions, I encourage practical community improvements supporting all. The new shelter represents my dedication ensuring families access stability as aided me. Integrated services will streamline stabilization journeys. Witness the facility's formation through generosity maintaining hope determinations coupled with care can overcome hurdles.

Visibly committing to "lifting up" Milwaukee revives motivation that one person's efforts spark change. My advocacy renews belief that dedicated individuals still fight boldly on vulnerability's behalf. Interest in my journey inspires knowing themes of persevering against adversity resonate universally. For all facing personal trials, my bettering myself and lives through resilience models striving as old as humanity. Preserving optimism that dark nights give way signifies this account's importance.

By vulnerably recounting hardships, readers form intimate bonds amplifying motivational impacts. This intimacy grants my triumphs added meaning as overcoming personal dragons collectively. My storytelling suggests transforming societies through shedding light in shared shadows. Ensuring struggling access stabilizing resources signifies my noblest triumph over adversity—sharing survival stories strengthens entire communities. I aim to aid all facing tribulations rise empowering others as champion despite darkness remaining guides into light. Preserving hope turns night into dawn for disadvantaged through memoirs ensures shining generations forward.

CHAPTER 10:

LEAVING AN INDELIBLE MARK

As I reflect on my life journey, filled with struggles, triumphs, and the resilience of the human spirit, I am compelled to share the valuable lessons I have learned along the way. In this final chapter, I want to emphasize the importance of being cautious and discerning regarding the people we surround ourselves with. Throughout my experiences, I have understood that not everyone has our best interests at heart, even those within our own families. It is crucial to be aware of this reality and learn how to navigate relationships wisely, as the wrong company can harm our lives.

In the depths of my memory lies the story of my battle with seizures. Growing up, I faced numerous challenges due to this condition, but the support of my loved ones and medical professionals helped me adapt and cope. However, not everyone in our lives will offer the same support and understanding. Some individuals, even those we hold dear, may let us down when we least expect it. It is essential to recognize this possibility and be prepared to accept it without letting it hinder our progress.

One incident that profoundly affected me was the tragic event involving my childhood friend, John, and a young boy in our neighborhood. John, who always carried a gun, allowed his anger to consume him, resulting in a devastating outcome. This experience taught me a valuable lesson about the importance of caution and non-violence. It is crucial to surround ourselves with individuals who share similar values and who encourage us to make wise choices. People who resort to violence can lead us down a destructive path, and we must steer clear of such influences.

Often considered a source of unconditional love and support, family can also be a complex web of dynamics. My own family had its ups and downs, and the loss of my oldest brother and mother created a void that could never be filled. I had to learn to navigate life without their guidance and support. It was a challenging journey, but I found solace in the memories of their love and care during my most difficult moments.

However, even within a family, there can be tension and discomfort. I experienced this firsthand when my oldest brother and his wife did not fully embrace my presence. It made me feel out of place and at times, unwanted. These experiences taught me that not everyone in our family circle will always understand or accept us for who we are. We must recognize these dynamics and find strength within ourselves to overcome their challenges.

Through it all, I have come to realize that while we may encounter disappointments and setbacks caused by others, it is crucial not to hold grudges or harbor ill feelings. The negativity that can arise from dwelling on these experiences will only hinder our own growth and progress. Instead, we must learn to accept the flaws and shortcomings of those around us, including our family members, and focus on our own personal development.

Throughout my journey, I have also discovered the importance of cultivating positive relationships with siblings and loved ones who genuinely care for us. My sisters and brothers played a vital role in supporting me during difficult times, and their presence provided a sense of comfort and connection. These relationships helped shape me into the person I am today, and I am grateful for their unwavering support.

However, we must remember that not everyone we encounter will have our best interests at heart. There will be individuals who try to bring us down or hinder our progress. It is crucial to be discerning, to recognize warning signs, and to distance ourselves from toxic influences. Surrounding ourselves with positive, uplifting people who genuinely want to see us succeed is vital for our personal growth and well-being.

The absence of a mother's love is a void that can be felt deeply, and it has a profound impact on our lives. Losing my mother at the tender age of 16 to breast cancer was a devastating experience that shook the foundation of my existence. During this time, I began to understand the complexities of human relationships and the dynamics that can arise when a mother figure is no longer present.

When a mother is no longer with us, many people may try to fill that void in various ways. Some individuals, driven by a sense of self-importance or a desire for control, may attempt to assert their influence over us, believing that we still need them in the absence of our mothers. They may try to manipulate situations or impose their opinions on us, all under the guise of caring for our well-being. However, often hidden beneath their actions is jealousy and envy, fueled by the fact that they are not our blood relatives and cannot replace the irreplaceable love of a mother.

These individuals can take various forms in our lives. It could be a partner, a girlfriend, or even friends who feel threatened by our growth and independence. They may use our lack of a mother's presence to exert control or make us feel indebted to them. They may constantly remind us of their presence, emphasizing that they are the ones who are there for us and use it as leverage in their favor.

Jealousy, as you mentioned, rolls deep into the hearts of these individuals. They observe our progress, resilience, and ability to navigate life without our mothers, and it stirs feelings of inadequacy within them. They may question why we can thrive and succeed even without a mother's support while they struggle to find their own sense of purpose and fulfillment. In their envy, they try to bring us down, belittle our achievements, and make us doubt our own capabilities.

It is important to recognize these behaviors and the motives behind them. While it may be tempting to seek validation and comfort from these individuals, we must remain grounded in our own strength and self-reliance. We must remember that the love and guidance of a mother cannot be replaced, and no one else can fill that void. It is crucial to find solace within ourselves and find ways to honor our mother's memory and teachings, even in her physical absence.

During my journey, I encountered individuals who tried to exploit my vulnerability, making me feel that I needed them. They would bring up their own mothers in conversations, using them as excuses for their actions or as a means to manipulate my emotions. However, I gradually realized that their intentions were far from genuine. They were merely using their mothers as a shield to deflect accountability for their own behavior and to maintain a sense of control over me.

These experiences taught me the importance of setting boundaries and recognizing when someone's intentions are not aligned with our well-being. It is essential to surround ourselves with people who genuinely support and uplift us rather than those who seek to exploit our vulnerabilities. Recognizing the toxic dynamics in these relationships and finding the strength to distance ourselves from them is crucial for our personal growth and happiness.

While the absence of a mother's love may leave us feeling vulnerable and longing for companionship, it is vital to remember that we can find strength within ourselves. We must not allow the absence of a mother to define us or limit our potential. Instead, we can draw upon the memories and teachings of our mothers to guide us, inspire us, and shape us into the best versions of ourselves.

In the face of adversity and challenges, it can be difficult to maintain a sense of hope and keep moving forward. However, certain principles and beliefs can guide us in our journey towards a brighter future. When it comes to finding hope and moving forward, three key pieces of advice have proven instrumental in my life.

The first piece of advice is to have faith in God. Undoubtedly, faith in a higher power can provide us with the strength and resilience needed to navigate life's trials. Through this unwavering belief in God's guidance and purpose, we can find solace in the midst of uncertainty. Trusting in a divine plan and surrendering our worries to a higher power allows us to let go of the burdens that weigh us down and opens the door for new possibilities to unfold.

However, faith alone is not enough. The second piece of advice is to have confidence in ourselves. It is important to recognize our own capabilities and worth. We must believe in our abilities to overcome obstacles and achieve our goals. This self-assurance empowers us to take action and move forward with determination. Without self-confidence, we may be held back by self-doubt and fear, hindering our progress. By embracing our inner strength and recognizing our potential, we can propel ourselves towards a brighter future.

The third and final piece of advice is to take action. Hope and faith must be accompanied by tangible efforts to bring about change. It is not enough to simply talk about our goals and aspirations; we must actively pursue them. By taking the necessary steps and putting in the hard work, we can create the conditions for success. It is through our actions that we manifest our hopes and dreams into reality. Moving forward requires us to be proactive, seize opportunities, and persist in the face of challenges.

I would like to express my deepest gratitude to God, my biggest adversary. Throughout my journey, it is God who has been my guiding light, my source of strength, and my constant companion. When faced with challenges and moments of despair, God's unwavering presence has provided me comfort and solace. His love and grace have sustained me through the darkest times and inspired me to keep moving forward.

While there may have been individuals who witnessed my struggles and successes, God has been the ultimate source of support and guidance. His unwavering presence and divine intervention have shaped my journey and enabled me to overcome obstacles. Through my faith in Him, I have found the strength to persevere and the hope to continue pushing forward.

In contemplating the impact my story and efforts will have on future generations, I aim to leave behind a legacy that instills a sense of hope, self-reliance, and determination. This ties back to the importance of having faith in God and relying on oneself, as mentioned earlier. By embodying these principles, I hope to inspire others to overcome obstacles and forge their own paths toward success.

The legacy I aspire to leave encourages individuals to have unwavering faith in God. Through my own experiences, I have witnessed the transformative power of trusting in a higher power. My sincerest hope is that by sharing my journey, others will be inspired to develop their connection with God and find solace in His guidance. I want future generations to understand that faith can serve as a steadfast anchor, providing strength and direction even in the most challenging times.

Equally important, I want to emphasize the significance of self-reliance and confidence. Throughout life, we encounter people who may doubt our abilities or withhold their support. However, I believe that true success lies in our own hands. By relying on ourselves and having unwavering confidence, we can overcome adversities and achieve greatness. I hope that my story will empower future generations to trust in their own capabilities and persevere despite any obstacles they may face.

It is crucial for individuals to understand that they are the architects of their own destinies. The support of others may come and go, but the belief in oneself should remain constant. I want future generations to embrace the notion that they have the power to shape their own lives. By maintaining a strong sense of self and staying motivated, they can overcome any setbacks and achieve their dreams.

In leaving this legacy, I also want to shed light on the reality that not everyone will be there to offer a helping hand. There will be moments when individuals face skepticism, judgment, or even betrayal from those closest to them. However, it is during these challenging times that one's faith in God and self-confidence become even more critical. I hope that future generations will internalize the importance of staying resilient and continuing to move forward, even when the support they expect is absent.

Ultimately, my desire is for the legacy I leave behind to serve as a guiding light for individuals navigating their own journeys. I want future generations to embrace the power of faith, self-reliance, and determination. By doing so, they can overcome any obstacles they encounter and lead fulfilling lives.

Writing this memoir has had a profound impact on me, both personally and emotionally. It has provided me with a deeper understanding of myself, the people around me, and the world at large. Documenting my life story has been a cathartic experience, allowing me to confront my past, find closure, and gain newfound wisdom.

The process of writing this memoir has allowed me to delve into the depths of my own experiences and emotions. It has forced me to confront moments of joy, pain, and vulnerability, as well as the choices I have made along the way. Through the act of putting my story onto paper, I have gained a clearer perspective on who I am and the events that have shaped me. This self-reflection has been both challenging and liberating, as it has enabled me to embrace my past and accept myself fully.

Moreover, writing this memoir has heightened my awareness of the people in my life. It has opened my eyes to the true nature of those around me, both within my family and beyond. Recounting my journey has made me more observant, allowing me to closely analyze people's actions, words, and intentions. It has made me more discerning, recognizing the signs of genuine support and the hidden agendas of those who wish to see me fail.

Through this memoir, I have come to understand that not everyone in my life is deserving of my trust. It has taught me the importance of being cautious, especially when it comes to those who claim to be friends or family. I have learned to be vigilant in assessing people's true intentions and to protect myself from those who may seek to exploit or harm me.

This newfound awareness has been both enlightening and challenging. It has forced me to reevaluate my relationships and to make difficult decisions about who I can truly rely on. While this process has been emotionally taxing, it has empowered me to surround myself with individuals who genuinely support and uplift me. It has also allowed me to distance myself from toxic influences, preserving my own well-being and sense of self-worth.

In addition to the impact on my personal relationships, writing this memoir has taught me invaluable lessons about human interaction. It has provided me with a deeper understanding of the complexities of human behavior and the importance of paying attention to subtle cues and signals. By observing how people respond to various situations and how they communicate, I have become more adept at discerning their true intentions.

This wisdom gained from my experiences and observations has become a guiding force in my life. It has helped me navigate through the intricacies of social dynamics, allowing me to make informed decisions about who to trust and who to avoid. Through this memoir, I hope to pass on this wisdom to future generations, enabling them to navigate their own journeys with greater insight and discernment.

CHAPTER 11:

THE PILLARS OF RESILIENCE

In the face of life's relentless challenges, resilience and determination have been my guiding lights, illuminating even the darkest moments. My journey has been marked by perseverance, an unyielding drive to overcome the obstacles life has thrown my way. One of the most profound lessons I have learned is the importance of education. Always educating oneself—whether through books, newspapers, or any form of reading—has been a cornerstone of my resilience.

As a child, I often found solace in the pages of a book. Reading became my refuge, a way to escape the harsh realities of my condition and the tumultuous environment around me. My mother, a beacon of wisdom, always encouraged me to pick up a book, to read anything that would enrich my mind. "The more you read, the more you learn, and the more you learn, the more you grow," she would say. And she was right. The habit of reading not only expanded my knowledge but also provided a sense of stability and control amidst the chaos of seizures and personal loss.

I vividly remember the days when I would sit by the window, a book in my hand, immersing myself in stories that transported me to different worlds. These moments were precious, offering a reprieve from the physical and emotional toll of my seizures. The act of reading, of continuously educating myself, became a form of self-care, a way to arm myself with knowledge and resilience. It taught me that no matter how insurmountable the challenges seemed, there was always a way to rise above them.

Faith and spirituality have also played a pivotal role in my journey. My faith in God has been a source of unwavering strength, a foundation upon which I have built my resilience. In times of despair, it was my faith that kept me grounded, providing a sense of purpose and hope. My mother instilled in me the importance of having faith, not just in God, but also in myself. "First, have faith in God," she would say, "and then have faith in yourself. Always have confidence that you can do anything."

This belief became a mantra for me, a guiding principle that helped me navigate the most challenging times. Without faith, without confidence, there is no movement, no progress. It is faith that propels us forward and gives us the courage to face our fears and persevere. In moments of doubt, when the weight of my condition felt too heavy to bear, it was my faith that lifted me, reminding me that I was never alone.

One of the most profound experiences that tested my faith was the tragic loss of my brother and mother. Their passing left a void in my life, a hole that seemed impossible to fill. But it was my faith that helped me endure, that provided a sense of peace amidst the grief. I found solace in prayer, in the quiet moments of reflection where I could connect with a higher power. It was in these moments that I felt a sense of calm, a reassurance that everything would be okay.

Faith also gave me the strength to believe in myself, to trust in my abilities and to persevere despite the odds. It taught me that confidence is essential and that without it, we are paralyzed by fear and self-doubt. This belief in oneself is crucial, especially in a world where we are constantly judged and compared to others. We live in a society where competition is inherent, where people are always trying to outdo one another. But true resilience comes from within, from the ability to remain steadfast in the face of adversity and to keep moving forward, no matter what.

Throughout my journey, I have drawn inspiration from various sources. One person who has significantly influenced me is Denzel Washington. His wisdom and resilience have been a beacon of hope, motivating me to keep pushing forward. I remember watching him on TV and listening to his words of encouragement. "Everybody can't go with you when you're on your way up," he said. "When you're moving up the ladder, you have to leave some people behind. Those who try to drag you down, let them go."

These words resonated deeply with me. They reminded me that not everyone would support my journey and that some people would try to hinder my progress. But it was essential to let go of negativity, focus on my path and keep moving forward. Denzel's experiences mirrored my own in many ways, and his resilience inspired me to stay strong, never look back, and always keep moving.

Another pivotal moment in my journey was the realization that I had to take charge of my destiny. With the loss of my mother and brother, I found myself alone, facing the challenges of my condition without their support. But this loss also became a turning point, a catalyst for growth. It taught me the importance of self-reliance of finding strength within myself. I had to become my own guardian to take responsibility for my well-being and future. It was a daunting task, but it also empowered me. I learned to be vigilant about my health, ensuring I took my medications on time and attended all medical appointments. It was a lesson in responsibility and discipline, one that has stayed with me throughout my life.

Despite the hardships, my journey has also been filled with moments of joy and triumph. I have come to cherish the good times, to find beauty in the simplest of things. The support of my family, especially my sister Babe, has been instrumental in this. After my mother and older brother passed away, Babe became my rock. I often sought comfort at her house, spending nights there when the loneliness became too overwhelming. Her unwavering support and love provided a sense of stability, a reminder that I was not alone in this journey.

One of the most significant lessons I have learned is the importance of self-motivation. Life is full of challenges, and there will always be obstacles in our path. But it is our determination and drive that enable us to overcome these hurdles. We must constantly push ourselves to be better to strive for excellence in everything we do. This mindset has been crucial in my journey, helping me to stay focused and motivated even in the face of adversity.

I have also learned the value of letting go. There are people and situations that can hold us back, that can drain our energy and hinder our progress. It is essential to recognize these negative influences and distance ourselves from them. This was a difficult lesson to learn but an important one. Letting go of toxic relationships and situations has allowed me to focus on my growth and well-being to surround myself with positivity and support.

My faith has been a constant source of strength, guiding me through the toughest times. It has taught me the importance of hope and perseverance, of believing in something greater than myself. This belief has provided a sense of purpose, a reason to keep pushing forward despite the challenges. It has also instilled in me a sense of gratitude, a recognition of the blessings in my life.

Gratitude has played a significant role in my resilience. It has helped me to focus on the positive aspects of my life to appreciate the support and love I have received from my family and friends. This mindset has been crucial in helping me to stay positive and motivated, even when faced with adversity. It has also reinforced the importance of giving back of supporting others in their journey.

One of the most profound experiences in my life was witnessing the tragic incident involving John and the young boy. This event left an indelible mark on my soul, a reminder of the fragility of life and the importance of making positive choices. It was a harrowing experience, one that tested my faith and resilience. But it also reinforced the importance of compassion and empathy, of understanding the struggles that others face.

I had to become my own guardian to take responsibility for my well-being and future. It was a daunting task, but it also empowered me. I learned to be vigilant about my health, ensuring I took my medications on time and attended all medical appointments. It was a lesson in responsibility and discipline, one that has stayed with me throughout my life.

Despite the hardships, my journey has also been filled with moments of joy and triumph. I have come to cherish the good times, to find beauty in the simplest of things. The support of my family, especially my sister Babe, has been instrumental in this. After my mother and older brother passed away, Babe became my rock. I often sought comfort at her house, spending nights there when the loneliness became too overwhelming. Her unwavering support and love provided a sense of stability, a reminder that I was not alone in this journey.

One of the most significant lessons I have learned is the importance of self-motivation. Life is full of challenges, and there will always be obstacles in our path. But it is our determination and drive that enable us to overcome these hurdles. We must constantly push ourselves to be better to strive for excellence in everything we do. This mindset has been crucial in my journey, helping me to stay focused and motivated even in the face of adversity.

Maintaining a positive mindset has been a deliberate and essential part of my daily routine. Every day, I make a conscious effort to keep my spirits high and my outlook optimistic. This isn't always easy, especially in a world where negativity can often overshadow the good. However, I have developed specific strategies that have helped me maintain a positive mindset.

Firstly, I am a motivator by nature. I motivate myself to keep it moving and keep it positive. In order to live a fulfilling life in a world that can often seem mad and chaotic, it's crucial to stay focused on the good. I see many people around me struggling, taking medications to manage their mental health issues. While these medications are necessary and life-saving for many, I also recognize the importance of self-motivation and positive thinking in managing my own well-being.

Without motivation, without having faith in God, and without having faith in myself, I don't know where I would be. Believing in yourself is fundamental. Without self-belief, it's difficult to achieve anything in today's world. I make it a point to remind myself every day of my worth and capabilities. This self-motivation is what keeps me moving forward despite the challenges that come my way.

To maintain a positive mindset, I have integrated several strategies into my daily routine. These strategies have been instrumental in helping me stay positive and resilient.

Daily Affirmations: Every morning, I start my day with positive affirmations. These are simple yet powerful statements that set the tone for the day. Phrases like "I am strong," "I am capable," and "I am worthy" help reinforce a positive mindset from the moment I wake up.

Gratitude Journaling: Keeping a gratitude journal has been incredibly beneficial. Every day, I write down at least three things I am grateful for. This practice helps me focus on the positives in my life, no matter how small they may seem. It shifts my perspective and reminds me of the blessings I have, even during tough times.

Physical Activity: Engaging in physical activity is another key strategy. Whether it's a brisk walk, a workout session, or simply stretching, physical activity helps release endorphins, which are natural mood lifters. It also provides a sense of accomplishment and boosts my overall well-being.

Mindfulness and Meditation: Practicing mindfulness and meditation has been transformative. These practices help me stay grounded and present, reducing anxiety and stress. Even a few minutes of meditation each day can make a significant difference in my mental state.

Connecting with Loved Ones: Staying connected with family and friends is vital. Their support and encouragement provide a sense of belonging and remind me that I am not alone. Regular phone calls, visits, and even virtual meetings help strengthen these bonds.

Creative outlets like writing and art have also played a significant role in my healing process. They provide a way to express my emotions and experiences, offering a sense of catharsis and relief. Engaging in creative activities has been a form of therapy, helping me navigate through my emotions and find peace.

I would feel comfortable sharing some of my creative works from this period. To be honest, I learned a lot just by deciding to write a book. When I reached out for help with writing, I learned so much about the process. Seeing how professionals write and put everything together on a piece of paper was an invaluable learning experience. It taught me the importance of structure, clarity, and expression in writing.

This tragedy taught me the value of forgiveness, of letting go of anger and bitterness. It was a difficult process, but it was essential for my healing. Forgiveness allowed me to move forward to focus on my growth and well-being. It also reinforced the importance of supporting others of being a source of strength and comfort for those in need.

This process was a learning journey in itself, one that opened up new avenues of personal growth and self-expression. By engaging with professional writers and observing their techniques, I gained a deeper understanding of how to convey my thoughts and emotions effectively. It was incredible to see how words could be woven together to create a narrative that was both compelling and reflective of my experiences.

Writing became a powerful tool for me. It allowed me to articulate feelings that were often difficult to express verbally. Through writing, I was able to process complex emotions and experiences, transforming them into something tangible and manageable. It provided an outlet for my thoughts, a way to release pent-up emotions and find clarity.

Art, too, played a significant role in my healing process. The act of creating something beautiful, whether it was a drawing, painting, or craft, brought a sense of accomplishment and joy. Art allowed me to explore different aspects of my personality and provided a visual representation of my journey. Each piece became a testament to my resilience, a reminder of my strength and creativity.

Collaborating with professional writers was an eye-opening experience. I observed their methods, learned about the importance of structure, and understood the nuances of effective communication. This collaboration was not just about creating a book; it was about gaining insight into the craft of writing and storytelling.

One of the most valuable lessons I learned was the importance of editing and revision. The initial draft is just the beginning; refining and revising are crucial steps in creating a polished and impactful piece of writing. This process taught me patience and attention to detail, skills that have been beneficial in various aspects of my life.

Books have always held a special place in my heart. They are a source of knowledge, inspiration, and comfort. In today's world, audiobooks have become increasingly popular, offering a convenient way for people to access literature. I learned about the significance of audiobooks and the impact they can have on readers. The ability to listen to a story while commuting, exercising, or relaxing at home has made books more accessible to a wider audience.

Creating a book and potentially turning it into an audiobook became a goal for me. I wanted to share my story, my journey, and the lessons I had learned with others. I believed that my experiences could offer hope and inspiration to those facing similar challenges. By putting my story out there, I hoped to connect with others and provide a sense of solidarity and support.

The journey of creating a book was both challenging and rewarding. It required dedication, perseverance, and a willingness to be vulnerable. Writing about personal experiences meant revisiting painful memories and confronting difficult emotions. However, it was also a cathartic process, one that allowed me to heal and grow.

I am grateful for the support and guidance I received from professional writers. Their expertise and encouragement were invaluable. They helped me shape my narrative, ensuring that my story was authentic and impactful. Through this collaboration, I learned the importance of storytelling and the power of sharing one's experiences.

The year 2003 was a pivotal period in my life that brought with it some of the harshest lessons about human relationships. Until then, I had always believed that the bonds of love, friendship, and family were unbreakable. However, life has its ways of revealing truths that we often don't want to see.

In this phase of my life, I learned the painful reality that people can turn their backs on you, regardless of who they are. Whether it's your wife, girlfriend, family member, or friend, people often have their own agendas. The relationships I thought were rock-solid were tested, and many crumbled under the pressure. It became clear that sometimes, people are just waiting for you to stumble, eager to see you fail.

This realization was not easy to come to terms with. The sense of betrayal cut deep, especially when it came from those I had once held close. But this period of disillusionment also taught me an invaluable lesson: the only person you can truly rely on is yourself. In understanding this, I began to cultivate a stronger sense of self-reliance and resilience.

One of the hardest pills to swallow was that even those who professed undying support could become distant when life got tough. I remember distinctly a time when facing a personal crisis, I reached out to someone I considered a close friend. Their response was not what I expected; instead of offering support, they seemed inconvenienced by my need. It was a turning point that made me question the authenticity of many relationships in my life.

This wasn't an isolated incident. Over time, I noticed a pattern: when I was at my lowest, the people I thought I could count on were often the first to disappear. It was a harsh lesson in the fickleness of human nature. The facade of companionship crumbled, revealing a stark reality that forced me to reevaluate who I allowed into my inner circle.

Despite the disappointment, this period also highlighted the true supporters in my life. My siblings, although we weren't always close, proved to be my pillars of strength. Being the youngest of six, I often felt a bit isolated, as there was a significant age gap between us. Yet, in my moments of need, they were there, offering the kind of support that only family can provide.

My sister Babe, in particular, became a confidante. We spent countless hours talking, her wisdom and experience guiding me through some of the darkest times. My brothers, too, played a crucial role, their presence a steady reminder that despite our differences, family ties run deep.

Growing up as the youngest in a large family had its unique challenges. The age gap between me and my older siblings often made it difficult to relate to them. It felt like I was navigating the world on my own, even though I had siblings. This dynamic taught me early on that having siblings doesn't necessarily mean you will be close.

Many people believe that having brothers and sisters guarantees a built-in support system. However, my experience taught me otherwise. Siblings have their own lives, their own struggles, and sometimes, their own issues with each other. It's a misconception to think that familial ties automatically translate to emotional closeness.

I learned to cherish the moments of connection with my siblings but also understood that I needed to be independent. This realization was crucial in developing my sense of self-worth and resilience. It's easy to fall into the trap of expecting others to be there for you simply because of familial bonds, but life has a way of teaching you that you must forge your own path.

One of the most important lessons I learned during this time was the importance of self-reliance. While it's comforting to think that others will always be there for you, the reality is that you must be your own greatest advocate.

This mindset shift was liberating. It allowed me to take control of my life in ways I hadn't before.

I began to focus on my own goals and aspirations, understanding that my success depended on my efforts. This period of self-discovery was empowering. It made me realize that while external support is valuable, the most crucial factor in my journey was my determination and resilience.

Navigating through these challenging times required a positive mindset. It's easy to become cynical when you feel let down by those you trust. However, I chose to focus on the positives. I realized that the setbacks and betrayals were opportunities for growth.

I learned to appreciate the small victories and the genuine connections I had. My relationship with my children became a source of immense joy and motivation. Their unconditional love and support were a reminder that, despite the disappointments, there were still beautiful aspects of life worth cherishing.

Setbacks are inevitable, right? Life is full of ups and downs, and it's how we respond to these challenges that define our journey. Seeing setbacks as stepping stones is key to progress. Each obstacle you face is an opportunity to learn, grow, and become stronger. How would I emphasize that? Well, I'd look at it like this: setbacks are not the end of the road but a part of the journey that shapes who we are.

In life, I learned that you don't lose; you learn. People come into your life for a reason, a season, or a lifetime. Some are there to teach you lessons, others to support you through certain phases, and a few will stand by you forever. Recognizing who fits into which category is crucial. It helps manage expectations and reduces the feeling of disappointment when relationships change or end.

Understanding that not everyone is meant to stay in your life forever is liberating. Some people are only with you for a season, and that's okay. They serve a purpose during a particular period, and when their role in your life is fulfilled, they move on. Others are there for the long haul, and these are the relationships worth investing in.

You're traveling alone in this world, and along the way, you'll meet many people. Some will be with you, and some will be against you. It's a reality we must face. Not everyone you meet is meant to stay, and not everyone will support your journey. This understanding is a stepping stone to building resilience. By learning to discern who is genuinely in your corner, you can focus your energy on nurturing those meaningful connections.

It's important to always keep in mind that everyone is not going to be for you. Everyone is not going to support your beliefs or aspirations. So, don't look forward to a lot of people believing in what you believe in and being down for you. Look forward to doing things yourself and achieving your goals independently. Whoever you meet, they're either going to be with you or against you. You must be watchful and wise in choosing your close circle.

What advice or perspectives would I impart to readers facing their own challenges? Life is full of demons—both literal and metaphorical. These demons can be internal struggles or external adversaries. People will try to hold you back, talk bad about you, and undermine your confidence. It's essential to recognize that these negative voices often stem from others' insecurities and internal battles.

People with their own internal demons will project their negativity onto you. They might talk bad about you, even to your face, or spread rumors behind you. Recognize that this is a reflection of their own issues, not yours. These challenges are designed to test your strength and resilience. It's crucial not to internalize their negativity. Instead, use it as fuel to propel yourself forward.

When someone says your book won't work or that you're not smart enough to succeed, understand that these are demons trying to challenge and break you. These voices are not truth, but obstacles meant to test your resolve. Every time you face such negativity, remember that it's a stepping stone—a chance to prove yourself and rise above.

One of the most empowering lessons is learning to rely on yourself. While having support is wonderful, your journey ultimately depends on your own efforts and perseverance. Always look forward to doing things for yourself and maintaining a positive mindset. Don't let anyone kill your self-esteem or confidence. Negative voices are often full of falsehoods, aiming to destroy your spirit. Recognize that it's a game designed to derail you from your path.

Maintaining a positive mindset is critical. Surround yourself with positivity, whether it's through uplifting books, supportive conversations, or spending time with people who encourage you. Gratitude can be a powerful tool in this regard. By focusing on what you have rather than what you lack, you cultivate a mindset of abundance and resilience.

It's also important to build a strong sense of self-worth. Know that your value is not determined by others' opinions but by your own beliefs and actions. When faced with challenges, remind yourself of your strengths and achievements. This internal validation is a powerful defense against external negativity.

We all face demons—whether they are internal struggles or external adversaries. People with their own issues will often project their negativity onto you. They might say things to undermine your confidence or belittle your dreams. Recognize that this is a reflection of their own insecurities, not a measure of their worth or capabilities. When someone tries to bring you down, understand that it's more about them than it is about you. Their words and actions are often driven by their own fears and doubts. Recognizing this can help you maintain your confidence and focus on your goals.

Self-validation is a powerful tool in overcoming challenges. It involves acknowledging your own worth and achievements without relying on external approval. When you validate yourself, you become less susceptible to the opinions and judgments of others. This inner strength allows you to stay committed to your path, regardless of the obstacles or negativity you encounter.

One way to practice self-validation is through positive affirmations. Remind yourself daily of your strengths, talents, and accomplishments. Reflect on the progress you've made and the challenges you've overcome. This practice can reinforce your self-worth and build your resilience.

While self-reliance is crucial, it's also important to build a supportive network. Surround yourself with people who genuinely care about you and your success. These are the individuals who will lift you up when you're down and celebrate your victories with you. They provide emotional support, encouragement, and constructive feedback.

However, be discerning about who you let into your inner circle. Not everyone who enters your life has your best interests at heart. Some may be there for selfish reasons or to take advantage of you. Trust must be earned, and it's important to set boundaries to protect your emotional well-being.

Setting boundaries is an essential aspect of maintaining healthy relationships. Boundaries help protect your time, energy, and emotional health. They ensure that you're not giving more than you can afford and that you're not being taken advantage of.

When setting boundaries, be clear and assertive. Communicate your needs and limits to others, and don't be afraid to enforce them. It's okay to say no and to prioritize your own well-being. Remember, those who truly care about you will respect your boundaries.

Challenges are inevitable, but how you perceive and respond to them makes all the difference. Instead of viewing challenges as obstacles, see them as opportunities for growth and learning. Each challenge you face is a chance to develop new skills, gain new insights, and become stronger.

For example, if someone criticizes your work, use it as an opportunity to improve. Constructive criticism can provide valuable feedback that helps you grow. Even negative criticism can teach you resilience and the ability to maintain your confidence in the face of adversity.

Resilience is the ability to bounce back from setbacks and keep moving forward. It's a quality that can be developed and strengthened over time. Cultivating resilience involves maintaining a positive outlook, staying flexible, and being persistent in the face of challenges.

One way to build resilience is by setting small, achievable goals. Each time you accomplish a goal, no matter how small, it boosts your confidence and reinforces your ability to overcome challenges. Over time, these small victories add up, creating a strong foundation of resilience.

Change is a constant in life. Whether it's a change in circumstances, relationships, or goals, it's something we all must navigate. Embracing change means being open to new possibilities and adapting to new situations. It involves letting go of what no longer serves you and making room for growth and new opportunities.

When faced with change, focus on the positive aspects and the potential it holds for your future. Instead of resisting change, see it as an opportunity to learn and grow. This mindset shift can make the transition smoother and more rewarding.

Vulnerability is often seen as a weakness, but it's actually a source of strength. Being vulnerable means being open and honest about your struggles, fears, and insecurities. It involves sharing your true self with others and seeking support when needed.

By embracing vulnerability, you build deeper connections with others. It allows you to form genuine relationships based on trust and mutual understanding. Vulnerability also fosters personal growth, as it encourages you to confront and overcome your fears.

Reflecting on my journey, I have come to realize that the path to personal victories and self-growth is often paved with the bricks of struggle and perseverance. Many people may not understand the depth of the battles I've faced, but through it all, there have been significant wins that I am immensely proud of—accomplishments that have shaped me into the person I am today.

One of the most significant achievements during this time has been the creation of this book. When the idea of writing a book was first presented to me, I never imagined how transformative the process would be. I am profoundly proud of this book, not just because it tells my story but because it represents a journey of learning and self-discovery.

When I embarked on this project, I knew very little about the intricacies of writing and publishing a book. However, I was determined to educate myself every step of the way. Working closely with those who helped me put this book together, I absorbed everything I could about the process. I studied my manuscript diligently, understanding the structure, the flow, and the importance of each word and sentence. This hands-on learning experience was invaluable.

Many people might hire someone to write a book for them and leave it at that, but I chose a different path. I didn't just want a book with my name on it; I wanted to understand the essence of creating a book. I wanted to know how to weave my experiences into a coherent narrative that could touch the hearts of readers. This commitment to learning and self-improvement is something I am incredibly proud of.

Through this process, I realized that you don't necessarily need formal education to achieve great things. While schools and universities provide valuable knowledge, some lessons in life can only be learned through experience. Writing this book taught me that self-education is a powerful tool. By immersing myself in the process, I discovered that I could learn and grow beyond what I thought was possible.

One of the most empowering aspects of this journey was the realization that learning is a continuous process. By studying my manuscript and working closely with those who guided me, I gained the confidence to pursue other goals and dreams. I learned that you must take responsibility for your own education and growth. No one else can do it for you. This book became a testament to my ability to persevere and overcome obstacles.

In sharing my story, I hope to inspire others to keep striving for their goals and dreams, no matter how daunting they may seem. My journey has not been easy—I have faced seizures, loss, and numerous challenges—but I have also experienced moments of triumph and personal growth. I believe that my story can serve as a beacon of hope for those who are struggling.

Overcoming seizures was one of the most significant victories in my life. It wasn't just about managing a medical condition; it was about reclaiming control over my life. Each seizure felt like a battle, but with each battle won, I grew stronger. The support of my family, especially my mother and brother, played a crucial role in helping me navigate this difficult journey. Their love and care gave me the strength to keep fighting.

But it wasn't just about overcoming seizures. Life threw other challenges my way—losing loved ones, navigating difficult family dynamics, and finding my place in the world. Each of these experiences taught me valuable lessons about resilience and determination. They showed me that no matter how tough the circumstances, there is always a way forward.

One of the key lessons I learned is the importance of having a strong mind. Overcoming obstacles requires mental fortitude and the ability to adapt to changing situations. Many people struggle to move past their challenges because they get stuck in a cycle of negativity. They repeat the same patterns day in and day out, unable to break free. But those who succeed are the ones who can push through and rise above their circumstances.

To achieve personal growth, you must be willing to confront your fears and tackle the obstacles in your path. It's about moving from level one to level two and beyond. Each level represents a new set of challenges but also new opportunities for growth. If you remain stuck on level one, you'll never realize your full potential. Overcoming challenges is the only way to become the person you were meant to be.

This journey has taught me that self-reliance is crucial. While the support of loved ones is invaluable, there comes a time when you must take charge of your own destiny. Losing my brother and mother was devastating, but it also forced me to become more independent. I had to learn to navigate life without their constant guidance and support. This was not an easy transition, but it made me stronger and more resilient.

My relationship with my siblings also evolved during this time. While there were moments of tension and difficulty, we managed to maintain a strong bond. The support and connection we shared helped me navigate the challenges I faced. It was a reminder that, even in the face of adversity, family can be a source of strength and comfort.

Looking back, I realize that every challenge I faced was instrumental in shaping my character and fortifying my resolve. The struggles, while painful, were necessary stepping stones that led me to a deeper understanding of life and myself. They taught me invaluable lessons about resilience, empathy, and the importance of perseverance.

One of the most poignant moments in my journey was witnessing the tragic incident involving John and the young boy. It was a harrowing experience that left an indelible mark on my soul. Yet, from this tragedy, I learned the profound impact of choices and the importance of advocating for peace and understanding. It reinforced my belief that violence is never the answer and that we must seek constructive ways to resolve conflicts.

As I navigated these turbulent times, I found solace in learning and self-improvement. The process of writing this book became a therapeutic exercise, allowing me to process my experiences and draw lessons from them. It was a reminder that, no matter how dire the circumstances, there is always a path to healing and growth.

The act of putting my story into words was empowering. It gave me a sense of purpose and a platform to share my experiences with others. Through this book, I aim to inspire readers to recognize their own potential and to believe that they, too, can overcome their challenges. My story is proof that, with determination and support, it is possible to rise above adversity and achieve great things.

I want readers to understand that personal growth is a continuous journey. It doesn't end once you've overcome a single obstacle. Life will always present new challenges, but each one is an opportunity to learn and grow. By embracing these challenges and viewing them as opportunities rather than setbacks, we can continue to evolve and reach new heights.

One of the key messages I hope to convey through this chapter is the importance of self-education. Formal education is valuable, but it is not the only path to knowledge and success. Many of the most important lessons in life can only be learned through experience and introspection. By taking an active role in our own education and growth, we can achieve things we never thought possible.

Writing this book has been one of the most rewarding experiences of my life. It has not only allowed me to share my story but also to learn about the intricacies of writing and publishing. I am proud of the knowledge I have gained and the skills I have developed. This experience has shown me that, with determination and a willingness to learn, we can achieve anything we set our minds to.

As I continue on my journey, I am committed to pursuing new goals and dreams. The lessons I have learned have equipped me with the tools I need to face future challenges with confidence and resilience. I am excited about the possibilities that lie ahead and am determined to make the most of every opportunity.

In sharing my story, I hope to inspire others to believe in themselves and to keep striving for their dreams. No matter how difficult the journey may be, remember that every challenge is an opportunity to grow and evolve. Embrace the struggles, learn from them, and use them as stepping stones to reach your full potential.

To those who are facing their own battles, I want to say this: You are stronger than you realize. The road may be tough, but you have the power to overcome any obstacle. Believe in yourself, seek support from loved ones, and never stop learning and growing. Your journey is unique, and your story has the potential to inspire and uplift others.

As I close this chapter, I am filled with gratitude for the experiences that have shaped me and for the people who have supported me along the way. My journey is far from over, and I am excited to see where it will lead. I am committed to living a life of purpose, growth, and resilience, and I encourage you to do the same.

Remember, the only limits that exist are the ones we place on ourselves. Break free from those constraints, embrace your potential, and keep striving for your dreams. Your story is still being written, and you have the power to make it a tale of triumph and inspiration.

Printed in the USA
CPSIA information can be obtained
at www.ICGtesting.com
LVHW051022221024
794501LV00020B/507